Gray Pancakes
and
Gold Horses

Kenneth Jernigan
Editor

Large Type Edition

A KERNEL BOOK
published by
NATIONAL FEDERATION OF THE BLIND

TABLE OF CONTENTS

Kenneth Jernigan, President Emeritus
National Federation of the Blind

EDITOR'S INTRODUCTION

This is the fourteenth volume in the Kernel Book series. Its title, *Gray Pancakes and Gold Horses*, is taken from the first two stories and symbolizes the theme of the book.

How do blind children learn the details of the hundreds of small daily acts that sighted children pick up without ever even knowing they have done it? A blind boy sits in a farm house on a summer night and wonders which way to shake his head to mean yes and no. He guesses and loses, and his mother's feelings are hurt. I know, for I was that boy.

A blind father cooks for his two sighted children, and the pancakes are gray, causing the children to reject them. Small incidents, things of no great moment. Yet, the stuff of daily living, the patterns and realities of life.

This Kernel Book is much like those that have gone before it. It contains first-person real-life stories, told by those who have lived them. It talks about going to school, communicating with others, and living from day to day. I know the people who appear in its pages. They are friends of mine. Some have been my students.

The one thing all of us who appear in this book have in common is our shared participation in the work of the National Federation of the Blind, the organization which has been the strongest single factor in making life better for the blind of this country during the twentieth century. With more than 50,000 members, the National Federation of the Blind is primarily composed of blind people, who are trying to make life better for themselves and other blind people, while at the same time making the world a better place in which to live for everybody.

We who are blind have a major job on our hands in trying to get members of the general public to see us for what we are—not especially blessed or especially cursed but just ordinary people, exactly like you. The only difference is that we don't have eyesight, which is not as big a factor in our daily lives as most people think it is.

So how do we get the job done? How do we get people to see us for what we are and not just what they have always thought we are? One of the most important ways is through the Kernel Books. This is why we write and publish them. They must be entertaining enough that people will read them, but they must do more than that. They must carry the message of what blindness truly is, and what it isn't.

We hope you will enjoy this book and that it will give you new insights about blindness. Since more than 50,000 people become blind in this country each year, the information you get from these pages may be useful to you in a personal way at some future time—and if not for you, then for a family member or friend.

As you read, remember that we who are blind have more hope today than ever before in history. We believe that when we can, we should do for ourselves before calling on others for assistance, but we also recognize the value of the help which a growing number of sighted friends and associates give us. We want to live the full lives of free, participating citizens, and we know that we can.

All of this you will see reflected in the pages of this book. We hope you will find it of interest and that it will cause you to rethink some of your notions about blindness.

Kenneth Jernigan
Baltimore, Maryland
1998

WHY LARGE TYPE?

The type size used in this book is 14 point for two important reasons: One, because typesetting of 14 point or larger complies with federal standards for the printing of materials for visually impaired readers, and we want to show you what type size is helpful for people with limited sight.

The second reason is that many of our friends and supporters have asked us to print our paperback books in 14 point type so they too can easily read them. Many people with limited sight do not use Braille. We hope that by printing this book in a larger type than customary, many more people will be able to benefit from it.

Kenneth Jernigan

and his mother, 1930

THE BARRIER OF THE VISIBLE DIFFERENCE

by Kenneth Jernigan

Catchy titles and clever phrases are the stuff of big business. As every advertising agency knows, fortunes are made or lost by the way the public reacts to a jingle or a slogan.

Once I heard a liquor distributor say that his company had a thoroughly mediocre wine that was going nowhere, and then somebody got the bright idea of giving it a sparkly name (I think it was Wild Irish Rose). After that, he said they couldn't make enough to meet the demand, operating three shifts a day.

Whether that story is true or false, the underlying message is right on target. It is not just what a thing is but how it sounds and feels that sets the tone and gives the value.

When most of us come across the term "visible difference," we think of the trademark of the beauty expert and cosmetics manufacturer Elizabeth Arden. "Visible Difference" is the brand name of moisturizers, lotions, and other products. But for the blind the term means something else. It represents a barrier and a hurdle to be surmounted. Let me illustrate.

When I was a boy of about four, my mother and I were sitting in the front bedroom of our home. Even though more than sixty-five years have passed, I still remember every detail. It was a summer evening just after dark. My father and brother were sitting on the porch, and the night sounds (the frogs and crickets) were coming into full chorus. It was oppressively hot with a lot of dust in the air.

In those days we didn't have electricity, so my mother had just lit the oil lamp. The smell of the burning kerosene began to blend with the regular odors of food and plant life that permeated the four-room house. Of course, all of the doors and windows were open.

When my mother finished lighting the lamp and adjusting the wick, she sat down and put her arm around me. Then she kissed me on the left side of my face. Since she was sitting on my left, this was a natural (almost an automatic) gesture. Then she said:

"Do you like for mother to kiss you?" Now, this put me into a real dilemma—for I very much liked for mother to kiss me, but I felt shy and embarrassed to say it.

Hunting a way out, I thought perhaps I could say yes by shaking my head. From conversations I had heard, I knew that other people shook their heads to mean yes or no, but I didn't know which way the head should move to indicate which meaning. It had never before occurred to me to wonder about the matter since I had never needed to know. My mother or anybody else around the house would undoubtedly have been perfectly willing to tell me if I had asked, but that didn't help in the situation I was then facing.

Using the best logic I could muster, I thought that since my mother was sitting on my left, maybe if I moved my head that way, it would indicate yes. Unfortunately it didn't, and my mother (not understanding my embarrassment and lack of knowledge) thought I was saying no. She was hurt and cried, and I didn't know how to explain.

So what is the moral of that little story, that minor tragedy of childhood? It is not that blind people are less competent than others of their age and circumstance. It is not that blind persons are slow learners or inept. It is that sometimes something that can be seen at a glance must be learned a different way by a blind person. The learning can be just as quick and just as effective, but it won't happen unless somebody thinks to explain, to help the blind child cross the barrier of the visible difference. There is no great problem in knowing how to shake one's head or in doing a hundred other things that sighted children learn without ever knowing that they have done it. It is only that the blind child must either be unusually persistent and inquisitive or have somebody constantly at hand who thinks to give information. Otherwise, insignificant details will multiply to major deficits.

And this is not just a matter of childhood. After seventy years I keep learning new things about the barrier of the visible difference. Recently when I told a blind friend of mine who is a lawyer about my head-shaking episode, he asked if I knew how you are supposed to hold your hand in a court when you are told to raise your right hand. I said that I had never thought about it but had always assumed that you simply raise your hand above your head, which is what would seem logical in the circumstances.

"No," he told me, "that isn't the way it is done. You raise your hand to shoulder level with the palm out." He went on to tell me that when he was being sworn in to be admitted to the Bar, he had raised his hand above his head and that later, one of his classmates had told him how the customary ritual is performed.

It is important to understand the significance of this incident. There is nothing better about raising the hand to the shoulder than over the head. It doesn't make one a better lawyer or a better witness in court. My friend is an excellent attorney, and I have testified in court on more than one occasion. We are simply dealing with a custom of society, a visible difference.

More than anything else (at least, unless one is aware of it and thinks about it) meaningless visible differences can lead to confusion and misunderstanding, and sometimes even to misplaced feelings of superiority or inadequacy. A thing that looks beautiful to the eye, for instance, can feel ugly and dirty to the touch. Again, let me illustrate. Once when I was four or five, my mother and father took me to the county fair. This was a big event.

We lived about fourteen miles from the county seat, and we didn't have a car. Very few people did in those days, so friends and neighbors pooled their transportation and helped each other with rides.

On this particular occasion my mother and I were standing at one of the booths at the fair. In retrospect it must have been one of those places that give prizes for throwing darts, tossing rings, or something of the sort. Regardless of that, the woman in charge gave me a small statue of a horse. As I think back on it, she may have done it because I was blind, or simply because she thought I was a cute kid. For purposes of my story, it doesn't matter.

The horse must have been quite pretty, for both the woman and my mother kept exclaiming about it. It was apparently covered with some sort of sparkly gold paint. To the eye I assume that it was extremely attractive, but to me it just felt dirty and grungy.

Now, I had never before had a small gold horse or, for that matter, any other kind of horse, or very many nice toys of any kind—

so I was pleased and ecstatic with my treasure. But I thought I ought to clean it up and try to make it look nice.

Therefore, while my mother and the woman were talking, I busily scratched all of the rough-feeling gold paint off of it. It was quite a job. By the time I had finished, my horse felt clean and attractive. I was proud of it. Imagine, then, my disappointment and chagrin when my mother and the woman noticed what I had done and were absolutely dismayed. I couldn't understand why they were unhappy, and they couldn't understand why I felt that the horse was better for my effort. Again, I had bumped head-on into the barrier of the visible difference.

Unlike the head-shaking incident, this was not exactly a matter of learning correct information. If a thing looks better to the eye and feels worse to the touch, that doesn't make it better or worse. It simply means a different point of view, a visible difference.

I thoroughly understand that we live in a world that is structured for the sighted, so if a blind person intends to get along and compete in society, he or she must learn how the sighted feel and what they think is beautiful and attractive. But this has nothing to do with innate loveliness or quality. It is simply a visible difference.

As a matter of fact, although I wouldn't scratch the paint off of it if I met it today, that horse of my childhood would feel just as dirty to me now as it did then. A few years ago when I went to Athens, I was invited (no, urged) to handle a variety of sculptures. They may have looked beautiful, and I have no doubt that they did; but they didn't feel beautiful—at least, not to me. They felt dirty, and I wanted a good hand-washing after feeling them. Hopefully this does not mean that I am either a barbarian or a boor, only that my way of appreciating beauty may have something to do with the fact that I touch instead of look.

Do not make the mistake of thinking that it is only the blind who get stuck on the barrier of the visible difference. The sighted do it, too—repeatedly, every day. Recently when I was in the hospital, I was being taken to the x-ray department for tests. On the way I had to stop to go to the bathroom. As I came out, a hospital official (I think she was a nurse) saw me and exclaimed, in what I can only describe as panic:

"Catch him! He's going to fall. His eyes are closed."

My wife explained to her that I am blind and that my eyes are usually closed. It made no difference.

"It doesn't matter," she said. "Hold him. His eyes are closed. He will fall." This woman is not abnormal or unusually jumpy, nor (at least, as far as I can tell) is she stupid. She is simply so accustomed to the fact that sighted people look about them to keep their bearings that she cannot imagine that sight and balance have nothing to do with each other. If I had thought it wouldn't have upset her, I would have asked her if she believed she would be unable to stand up in a totally dark room.

During that same hospital stay, when I stepped into another bathroom, the nurse turned the light on for me even though I told her in a light and pleasant tone that I didn't need it. She said she would turn it on anyway. It was clear that she felt uncomfortable to have me in the bathroom in the dark. Obviously this is not a major matter. It simply shows that we feel uneasy when something violates (even benignly) our routine patterns.

And these are not isolated instances. Every day letters and articles come to my attention to prove it.

A journalist from Ohio writes to say that the blind need special fishing facilities— and he will lobby the government to help make it happen. He doesn't say why we can't fish in the regular way like everybody else, which many of us do all of the time.

A locksmith from Wisconsin believes the blind would benefit from specially shaped door knobs (oval and textured, he thinks), and he is willing to design them. A pilot from Pennsylvania thinks we should solve any problems we have with the airlines by setting up an airline of our own, and he will help fly the planes.

A man from Minnesota believes that blind alcoholics cannot benefit from regular programs used by the sighted and suggests separate services. Some years ago the *Manchester Union Leader*, one of New Hampshire's most prominent newspapers, said that the governor of the state was so bad that only the deaf, the dumb, and the blind could believe he was competent.

These few illustrations are not a complete list, of course, but only a sampling. Moreover, I am not talking about all of the sighted. An increasing number are coming to understand and work with us. They give us some of our strongest support.

Nor am I saying that the sighted are hostile toward us. Quite the contrary. Overwhelmingly the members of the sighted public wish us well and have good will toward us. It is simply that they are used to doing things with visual techniques, and when they look at a blind person, they see something to which they are not accustomed—what I call the barrier of the visible difference.

Most sighted people take it for granted that doing something with eyesight is better than doing it some other way. Visual techniques are sometimes superior to non-visual techniques, and sometimes not. Sometimes the non-visual way of doing a thing is better. Usually, however, it isn't a matter of better or worse but just difference.

This brings me to my experience with the National Federation of the Blind. I first became acquainted with the Federation almost fifty years ago, and it has done more than anything else in my life to help me gain balance and perspective—to understand that the barrier of the visible difference need not be a major obstacle, either for me or my sighted associates.

With more than fifty thousand active members throughout the nation, the National Federation of the Blind is leading the way in making it possible for blind people to have normal, everyday lives. We of the Federation seek out parents and help them understand that their blind children can grow up to be productive citizens. We work with blind college students, giving scholarships and providing successful role models. Blind seniors make up an important part of the organization, helping and encouraging each other and exchanging ideas and information. We develop new technology for the blind and assist blind persons in finding jobs.

All of this is what we of the National Federation of the Blind do to help ourselves and each other, but the chief value of the organization is the way it helps us look at our blindness and the way it helps sighted people understand and accept. We who are blind know that with reasonable opportunity and training we can earn our own way in the world, compete on terms of equality with others, and lead ordinary, worthwhile lives. We do not feel that we are victims, or that society owes us a living or is responsible for our problems. We believe that we ought to do for ourselves and that we also should help others. These attitudes are the heart and soul of the National Federation of the Blind. They constitute its core beliefs and reason for being.

We go to meet the future with joy and hope, but we recognize that we need help from our sighted friends. If we do our part, we are confident that the needed help will be forthcoming. We also know that both we and the sighted can surmount the barrier of the visible difference and reduce it to the level of a mere inconvenience.

Marc and Patricia Maurer on the front porch of their home with children David and Dianna.

GRAY PANCAKES AND THE GENTLEMAN'S HAT

by Marc Maurer

How important is appearance? More than most people think. As readers of the Kernel Book series know, Marc Maurer is not only the President of the National Federation of the Blind but also the father of two sighted children, David and Dianna. The Maurers, like others who are blind, keep bumping into the matter of appearances. Here is what President Maurer has to say about it:

I have been given (along with almost everybody else I've ever met) the advice that I should not judge a book by its cover—that the intrinsic value of a thing is more important than its appearance—or that beauty is only skin deep. The problem with most of the people who have given me this advice is that they ignored it themselves much of the time. Those who try to live so that they may disregard the covers of books or the packaging on the outside of a commodity or the stylish cut of somebody else's clothes, are regarded as crazy and ostracized.

While I was a boy, attending the School for the Blind, I was forcibly made to realize the difference between the way a thing looks and the way it feels. The School for the Blind collected blind children from all over the state of Iowa, and we attended classes together. The boys living in dormitories were divided by age. The Cottage was a building for the little boys—the kindergartners and first graders. The second and third graders got to move into one wing of the boys' dorm. This was a major step in our growing up. When we lived in the Cottage, we attended classes and ate our meals in the Cottage. The classrooms and dining room for the small boys were all in the same building.

However, when we got to the second grade, we had begun to be counted among the bigger boys. We slept in the boys' dormitory, but we attended classes and ate our meals in the administration building.

One of the Saturday morning rituals for the boys in the fifth and sixth grades at the School for the Blind was shoeshining. We did this in the janitor's room. Each boy was required to have a can of shoe polish—cost, ten cents. A dauber, a shoebrush, and a polishing cloth were provided. I wasn't all warmed up about the shoeshining assignment because anything that interferes with the enjoyment of free time on a Saturday for a fifth grader is bothersome. However, I thought if I got the polishing out of the way, I could go somewhere else; so I started in with a will.

I soon discovered that polishing shoes has its disadvantages. I daubed the polish onto the leather, rubbed the shoes with the shoebrush for a time, and followed up with the polishing cloth. The shoes felt perfectly clean and smooth to me. I figured that I had finished the job and could go my way. But this was not the case. The house parent, the master of the shoeshining and general arbiter of boys' lives, came to inspect. The shoes were not shiny, he said. I was told to begin again. So, I started once more—this time with extreme care. I put on more polish, making certain it covered every part of the leather. I rubbed vigorously with the brush, and then I took up the polishing cloth. I polished diligently for a time, and I thought that they must certainly be done by now! But the inspector, the house parent, informed me that I had failed a second time. I started polishing my shoes for the third time and wondering whether I would be through polishing before lunch.

After the third try (another failure), the house parent asked an older boy to show me what to do. He took the polishing cloth and made a few swift passes over the shoes. Then he said, "See how easy that is?" I couldn't figure out why his polishing worked but mine didn't. From the perspective of many years, I have concluded that the speed of his polishing put the final shine on the shoes. They felt the same after I had polished them as they had after his effort. But they didn't look the same, and I understood the importance of getting them to look right.

The next step was to clean my hands. During the first attempt at polishing, I had kept my fingers out of the can of polish and away from the moist surfaces of the shoes. But when my polishing job was rejected, I decided that my fingers must tell me how much polish was being applied. My hands carried the unmistakable evidence; my fingers, my nails, and my knuckles were black. Shoe polish is intended to be reasonably waterproof. I washed my hands thoroughly; they felt perfectly clean to me. However, they were still black, and I was sent back to the basin to wash a second time. After several sudsings, my hands became clean; and I understood for the second time that the way a thing feels isn't the same as the way it looks.

Today, I know that appearance is important. The substance of a thing is more important, but often we don't explore the substance unless the initial appearance is attractive.

As readers of the Kernel Books know, my children, David and Dianna, are sighted. My wife and I are both blind. Much of the time we do not discuss the subject of blindness or its implications, but sometimes the difference in approach taken by a blind person from that of the sighted is significant.

I do much of the cooking for our household. One evening I decided to make potato pancakes for supper. This requires taking fresh potatoes and grinding them up before mixing them with flour, salt, and other ingredients to make pancake batter. When the pancakes are fried crisp and hot (and served with apple sauce, sour cream, or fruit compote), they are delicious. Most people peel the potatoes before grinding them up for the batter. However, I thought that I would grind the potatoes with their skins. Potato skins, I have been told, are very good for you—they contain all the vitamins and minerals.

Soon I had a nice pile of potato pancakes, crisp and hot. I called the family to eat them, but my children would not take the first bite. My wife and I thought the pancakes tasted just right, but we couldn't tempt the children. When I asked why, David gave me the answer. My pancakes were gray. Apparently, not peeling the potatoes before putting them in the pancake batter makes the pancakes come out gray, and gray pancakes are not very appetizing in appearance. They tasted great, but they looked awful. So, the children ate chicken noodle soup, and my wife and I finished the pancakes. Since that time, I have considered (even if fleetingly) both the appearance and the flavor of the things I cook.

As I have said earlier, I believe that appearance counts. My experience tells me that those who are most conservatively dressed are often taken most seriously. I dress conservatively, wearing white shirts, black wing tip shoes, and dark suits. A number of years ago, a friend took me to get a wool top coat. She told me that the winter coat I had been wearing was not suitable and that I needed a gentleman's coat. Along with the coat I obtained a pair of black gloves. However, I was never sure how to complete the ensemble. What should I wear for a hat?

I grew up in the state of Iowa, which frequently has a cold winter. As a boy, I was given a jacket with a hood. I disliked the hood because when I wore it, I had trouble hearing. I used my hearing to learn about my surroundings and to help me in traveling with my cane. A stocking cap is much better than a hood. It can be worn so that it completely covers my ears without interfering with my ability to hear.

My stocking cap became my good wintertime friend. I did cause myself trouble with it one time. On a particularly cold day, I pulled it down over my face. A stranger apparently felt outrage at my appearance. He said that I looked like a fool, and perhaps I did. After that, I wore the stocking cap in the customary manner, and I had no more trouble. However, a stocking cap would not do with my gentleman's coat.

I went to a hat shop to look at all the hats, and I asked for lots of advice. I finally selected a black felt Saxon style with a black band. I was told that it was exactly the right kind of hat to go with the gentleman's coat. I bought it mostly for style, but I hope that it also has some practical use as well. I am now learning about the language of the hat. For example, what does it mean to "tip" a hat, and when should the "tipping" occur? What other odd customs are associated with the hat, and how will I come to learn them?

If the purpose was to keep my head warm, I would go back to the trusty old stocking cap. But the purpose is to combine a practical function with the proper appearance.

In the National Federation of the Blind, we are doing what we can to help blind people become a meaningful, contributing part of our society. In order to make a contribution, we must learn enough so that the talent that we possess is useful. However, talent is not enough. We must also present the appearance of talent, and we are helping each other gain the proper appearance. Some people think our method of traveling from place to place with a cane or dog is odd or that some of the other alternative techniques used by blind people of performing ordinary tasks are unusual. Because some of the methods that we use to do ordinary things seem unfamiliar, some sighted people seem to feel uneasy in the presence of a blind person. Of course, there is no need to feel this way. Some of what we do is unconventional, but we have the same hopes and dreams, the same fears and frustrations, the same willingness to work and longing to make contributions that others have.

Through the National Federation of the Blind we are focusing this willingness to work and longing to contribute, and we are helping the dreams of blind people come true. We will do our best to remember that the pancakes should not be gray, and we will tip our hats at the proper time.

WHERE ARE THE EYES?

by Bruce A. Gardner

Bruce Gardner, active in the Mormon Church and President of the National Federation of the Blind of Arizona, is a successfully practicing lawyer in Phoenix, Arizona. Like many of us who are blind, he has had to learn through painful experience the importance of appearance and the symbols of successful behavior. Of course, nothing substitutes for performance and substance—but symbols count, more than is generally understood. Here is how Bruce tells about one of his experiences in moot court:

Should we who are blind be concerned with our posture, gestures, and facial expressions? If we do pay attention to these things, aren't we just trying to hide our blindness by pretending that we can see? I remember pondering these questions as a blind student in college.

My major was interpersonal communications, which included a wide variety of topics from debate and public speaking to family counseling and organizational communications. I found it interesting and a great preparation for life and the practice of law. As part of the major, I took several nonverbal communication classes in which we discussed how things other than spoken words (such as the voice and body language) affect the message that is conveyed. We studied the effects of inflection, pitch, tone, cadence, volume, and intensity of the voice, as well as gestures, posture, and facial expressions. We noted that variations in the voice can alter or even reverse the meaning of words. For example, "thanks a lot" can express genuine appreciation; however, if said with icy sarcasm, the message might actually be one of contempt.

Likewise in our predominantly sighted society, body language along with the voice affects the meaning of the spoken word. A friend may say she is happy and even do it with a cheerful tone in her voice, but the frown on her face and the droop in her shoulders may suggest otherwise. I learned that although

*In the courtroom or with his family Bruce
Gardner is in charge.*

as a blind person I may be unaware of the messages conveyed by body language, most sighted people (usually subconsciously) pay attention and give credence to the messages conveyed through gestures, posture, and facial expressions. For example, if I am facing away or looking down at my shoes when talking to someone, he may get the impression that I am not interested in him or what he has to say. I learned that it is therefore important to understand basic body language and use it properly when we are communicating in order to convey the intended message rather than mixed or incorrect messages.

Even so, communication is an art, not an exact science, and the best intentions can sometimes fall short. I vividly recall a situation in law school when that happened to me. I was selected to be on the moot court team representing the Brigham Young University Law School in intercollegiate moot court competition.

Similar to an undergraduate debate team, moot court competition consists of drafting a court of appeals brief and then arguing the case before a panel of judges. In intercollegiate competition a hypothetical legal issue and fact scenario is selected for the year. The moot court teams, consisting of three members each, are assigned to write a brief for the United States Supreme Court representing either the appellant or appellee in the hypothetical case. A great deal of legal research and analysis is done by the team members in selecting just the right cases to cite and legal arguments to make in each brief. The briefs are then carefully analyzed, critiqued, and scored.

Two members of each team then give oral arguments before a panel of judges just as if they were arguing the case before the Supreme Court. Although each team prepared its brief for either the appellant or appellee depending on the assignment, at oral argument the team must be prepared at the flip of a coin to argue the case for either side. The issues are divided in half, with one of the team members prepared to present oral argument for the appellant on one half of the issues and another team member prepared to present oral arguments on the other side of the case for the appellee on those same issues. The third member of the team is the swing member who must be ready to present the other half of the issues for either the appellant or the appellee. This meant that the swing member gave oral arguments each time the team competed, sometimes on one side of the case and sometimes on the other. Just before time to present oral arguments, with a flip of the coin, we would find out which side of the case we would be presenting. Because I had won the Dean's Cup that year for best oralist at the Brigham Young University Law School, I served as swing member of my team.

In regional moot court competition each law school in the region sends its two teams to the day-long multi-round competition. Each panel of judges is comprised of three practicing attorneys who live and work in the city where the host law school is located. In the semi-final round of regional competition, my team (which had gone undefeated to that point) faced the host law school's remaining team. Each presenter was interrupted numerous times by the judges asking pointed and difficult questions, and each oralist deftly fielded the questions and made compelling presentations.

After the semi-final round was finished, the two teams sat quietly in the courtroom awaiting the judges' verdict as to which team had won. We all knew each of the oralists on both teams had done extremely well and the scoring would be close. We also knew that if the scoring of the oral arguments was tied, my team would be declared the winner because our written brief had taken first place in the region.

When the panel of judges returned, they each gave a critique of our arguments. Each judge identified strengths and weaknesses of the presentations. After the first two critiques, it was apparent that the scoring was tied. We all wondered what the third judge would say, particularly because he had not opened his mouth or asked a single question during the entire semi-final round. The third judge made rather routine comments about each presentation, but then to my surprise and great dismay he had an additional unusual and negative criticism for me. He said that although my presentation was excellent and my arguments compelling, I did not look him in the eyes and convince him that I was right.

He further said that the fact that he had not asked a single question should not matter, and I should have looked him in the eyes and talked directly to him just as much as I did the other two judges. He then "docked" my team, which meant that the team from the host law school won by one point.

My teammates and I came away from that experience convinced of two things. First, the judge had no clue that I was blind, and he was therefore not trying to discriminate against me. After all, he had no opportunity to see my cane because we simply stood when the judges entered the courtroom and stood when they left, and I did not need or utilize my cane when I stepped from the table where I was sitting to the podium to give my presentation. And second, he (probably subconsciously) had decided that the home town team should win, and he caused that to happen in the only way he could think of. We knew this second notion was probably just sour grapes, but it made the losing more palatable.

The ironic thing was that harkening back to my non-verbal communication classes, I had made a conscious effort to look all three judges in the eyes, but because the third judge never said a word, I was not sure exactly where he was sitting or where to look. I was pretty sure he was to the right of the other two judges who frequently interrupted my presentation to ask me questions, so I would look in that general area occasionally during my oral argument, but to no avail. Oh well, as I said, communication is an art, not an exact science. You win some, and you lose some.

This incident reminded me of a conversation I had in one of my nonverbal communication classes taken several years earlier in undergraduate school. One day we were discussing various studies that addressed eye contact: how far apart people are when their eyes meet as they approach each other; how long it is customary to look a friend, stranger, subordinate, or superior in the eyes before glancing away; how often during a conversation direct eye contact is repeated; and the various messages that are conveyed by these actions.

One of the students said that he had noticed that the blind guy in the class (me) looked people in the eyes when he talked to them and he wondered why since he knew I could not see them. I responded by turning my face to the wall and saying, "Because it would look strange if I talked to you like this." He then said, "Yeah, but you look people right in the eyes. How do you know where to look?" I teasingly responded, "I don't know about you, but most people's eyes are just above their mouths; therefore, I use your voice to determine where to look." The whole class laughed.

Later, however, I did some serious reflecting on his question. Why did I face people when talking to them, and why did I pay attention to my gestures and facial expressions? Was it because I was still trying to hide my blindness by pretending that I could see and was "normal" as I had done for so many years before I learned the truth about blindness from the National Federation of the Blind?

It was only a couple of years earlier that I had learned of the NFB and begun accepting and dealing with my blindness. Before that time I had been ashamed of my blindness because I thought blind people were fumbling, bumbling Mr. Magoos or worse, virtually helpless dependents who sold pencils on the street corner. I did not want to be thought of like that, so I tried to hide my blindness. And of course, I did not use a cane.

I did crazy things to appear "normal." I came to think of these actions as playing "blindman's bluff." I would do ridiculous things, such as pretend to be reading a magazine in the barber shop or a doctor's office and turn the pages after the appropriate passage of time; loiter in lobbies outside what I hoped were the restrooms (sometimes in increasing discomfort) in order to identify a man and then observe which door he went through so I could follow him into the correct restroom; and pretend to be distracted or unfriendly rather than let people know I did not see or recognize them.

But now that I had learned the truth about blindness, that it is respectable to be blind, and was carrying a rigid long white cane like a neon sign that said "look at me, I am blind," hiding my blindness by pretending to see was not only impossible but out of the question.

Before I heard of the NFB my actions were motivated by my intent to con or deceive others into thinking I could see. But upon introspection I realized that thanks to the NFB, my motives had changed, and I was now simply trying to be a better communicator. I realized that there is a profound difference between trying to hide the fact that you are blind by pretending to see, and understanding and using body language as an important part of communication.

Barbara Pierce using her "Educated Fingers."

EDUCATED FINGERS

by Barbara Pierce

Barbara Pierce is the wife of a college professor, the mother of three children, the editor of the leading magazine in the blindness field, and the President of the National Federation of the Blind of Ohio. As indicated in the following article, she leads a full and active life. Here is what she has to say about some of her experiences.

From the time my daughter Anne was a tiny child she has had a sharp eye for detail. Before she could speak, she could point correctly to where I stored each piece of kitchen equipment. If there was a coin on the sidewalk or a four-leaf clover in the lawn, she would find it.

Since her marriage she has been working in the local jewelry store. Her gift of visual observation is now being trained in very specific ways. Her eyes are being educated to notice and appreciate subtle detail and to draw conclusions from what she sees.

Everyone who is neither blind nor colorblind can distinguish colors, but artists, interior decorators, and house painters notice shades and blend and contrast them with a sureness unmatched by the rest of the population. Similarly, auto mechanics, musicians, and linguists in very different ways have educated their ears to notice subtle differences in pitch and tone that escape the rest of us.

In the same way, while learning to function efficiently, a person who has become blind or a blind child must actually educate his or her fingers to discern nuance and appreciate small variations. As a young child I remember often being confused when I was handed unfamiliar objects. It took time and patience to learn to sort the shapes and make sense of what I was holding.

Take cookie cutters for example. The star, valentine, and Christmas tree were easy to identify. The gingerbread man, Santa Claus, and angel were almost as obvious. Animals were a little trickier. The Easter Bunny and chicken were simple, but I had trouble distinguishing between the dog and the sheep.

Then one day some friends handed me a cookie and asked if I could identify the shape. It was unlike anything I had ever handled. All the lines seemed to sweep in one direction, and one portion reminded me vaguely of a robe or skirt. I had not the remotest idea what the thing could be, but I felt great pressure to make a guess, and I was afraid of making what they would consider an absurd mistake.

In desperation I said, "a girl airplane." I knew perfectly well that aircraft did not have gender, but I hoped by making up an answer that was patently absurd to protect myself from being laughed at for making an actual mistake. To my surprise, they burst into delighted laughter and announced that my guess was more or less right. The cookie was a witch flying on a broomstick. I considered myself extremely lucky.

At the same time I recognized that a whole new range of outlines had just opened to me. I was used to identifying the shapes of objects standing still, looking like Christmas stockings or birds or cows. Suddenly I realized that lots of things moved and therefore could be depicted in motion and that I would have to build that concept into my efforts to recognize the shapes of things.

Having a visual knowledge of shape does not, however, translate directly into tactile understanding. Last Christmas my daughter Margy gave me a wooden puzzle of the United States in which each piece is a state. I had never had access to such a map as a child and had always wanted to know more particularly how the various states fit together.

As an elementary school teacher Margy knew where to find the puzzle, and I thoroughly enjoyed learning to assemble it. It took a weekend of intermittent fiddling to be able to identify all the states. After watching me explore the puzzle pieces, Margy decided to try putting it together with her eyes closed.

Of course she had the advantage of knowing the map well to begin with, but she was surprised to discover that she could not immediately identify many of the states by touch even though she had a mental image of what she was looking for. She is bright and as the daughter of a blind woman has had lots of tactile experience, so she mastered the skill quickly.

Like all other kinds of education, educating the fingers takes practice. But the more experience they get, the more easily fingers learn. Often you don't even realize how much your fingers know until they are put to the test.

When my children were small, I came home one day to discover that the baby-sitter had not kept as close tabs on the three as I could have wished. The labels had systematically been removed from all my canned goods. I have never bothered to label my cans in Braille as I would if I lived alone or with another blind person. I can usually identify the can I want by knowing its size and shaking all the cans of the right dimensions. When I ask a member of the family to confirm my choice, I am pretty frequently confirmed in my choice.

It is one thing to have your guesses confirmed by having someone read a label and quite another to check your guess by opening the lid and living with the consequences. On the whole, however, I did pretty well in this emergency. There was no way to distinguish among the various kinds of condensed cream soups, but pumpkin, kidney beans, and black olives all sound different from each other when shaken.

Folks often assume that blind people depend on always having things returned to their original position in order to manage their lives. There are certainly advantages to being able to glance around a room and see where your toddler has shed her socks or the dog has dropped your slipper. But actually in our household and among my friends I am often the one to find things that have gone missing.

One day I was out with a friend who had dropped her car key into her purse, but when we were ready to leave, she couldn't find it. She searched and researched her handbag and then got out and began looking on the ground around the car. I picked up her bag and fished out the key in about ten seconds. It had fallen into a letter. As soon as I moved the folded sheet, I knew it was too heavy to be a single piece of paper. When I slipped my fingers across the surface of the letter, I felt the outline of the key. She had been so busy looking for the key that she had not paid attention to what her fingers were telling her about the weight and balance of the paper.

Having educated fingers provides wonderful benefits. When our children were babies, I could get up at night and feed and change them without ever opening my eyes or waking up fully. The disadvantage was, of course, that my husband had a strong argument for giving me the lion's share of the night duty.

One of the reasons we bought our current home was the fireplace in the dining room. We were assured that it functioned well, but when we tried to build our first fire, we discovered that the damper, which was obviously quite new, would not open. The previous owner had repaired the fireplace and then not used it for years. Debris had sifted down over time and now prevented the damper from swinging open.

I covered the screen with a drop cloth and reached through with one hand. Working back-handed, I forced the damper open enough to slip my fingers through. Then I began flicking bits of ash, brick, and bird's nest out through the slit and eventually, as the damper opened wider, through the widening crack on the hinge side. It was hard work, and I banged up the backs of my hands and fingers, but I was eventually successful in freeing the damper so that we could use the fireplace.

Even though I had a little vision when my mother taught me to iron, I could not see the wrinkles in the pieces I was working on. From the first I had to learn how to smooth a panel of the garment and work close to the iron without burning myself. Though most sighted people don't believe it, this is actually quite easy to do. Now my favorite time to iron during the summer is late in the evening when a breeze blows through the windows of the converted sleeping porch that is my laundry room. I can read a talking cassette book in the darkness and iron while the birds go to bed and the crickets begin their chorus.

Our neighbors seem finally to have adjusted to the fact that I often weed the lawn and flower beds beginning at twilight. At first they questioned me about what I was doing sitting in the middle of my lawn in the dark and listening to a cassette book. Buckets of dandelions and ground ivy have convinced them that I actually am accomplishing something useful out there in the cool of the evening.

I was not always so comfortable letting others observe how I do things. Society exerts lots of pressure on blind people to do things like everybody else. It was members of the National Federation of the Blind, at ease with who they were and how they did things, who taught me that it was far better to get things done efficiently than to look like everybody else while I did nothing. This attitude makes eminently good sense, but it helps to know that members of the general public are now reading books like this one and learning why I search for things with my educated fingers and, as often as not, find them.

LET THE MEDALS JINGLE

by Tonia L. Valletta

Tonia Valletta is a superb gymnast. She has also found and come to realize the importance of the National Federation of the Blind. Here is what she has to say about both:

I remember how surprised I was when, during my eighth grade year, a fellow student in my Spanish class approached me and said admiringly, "Hey, I was doing some research, and I found a picture of you in *National Geographic World* magazine. I didn't know you used to do gymnastics!" My Mom has collected all the newspaper articles about me since I was three years old; they are tangible proof that being blind, let alone a blind gymnast, is a big deal to the rest of the world. But, it was not the numerous articles, the swell of being notorious, the people who said, "'You've inspired me so much," or the medals and ribbons that I loved so dearly: it was being a gymnast.

Mr. Roltsch was the coach who agreed to take me into his gym and teach me gymnastics when I was seven or eight years old. "I had never taught a blind gymnast before," he told me later, "so I was hesitant and a bit skeptical when your Mom called me and asked me to teach you. But, when your Mom brought you over, and I took you down into the gym to test you out, I decided it was worth the challenge to take you on as a pupil." He had a deep, powerful voice that I was drawn to because it said, "I expect 100 percent grit from you, and if you don't give it to me, I will be disappointed." At the same time, his voice was gentle and reassuring. He never hesitated to correct me, and he had a not-so-subtle way of telling me when he knew I was cheating him out of valuable time by slacking off. I rejoiced at every compliment I got from him, for he gave them only when my performance was nearly-perfect enough to merit them.

Mr. Roltsch was a demanding coach and a darn good one. Those of us on the team who appreciated gymnastics as both a sport and an art, just as Mr. Roltsch did, gave him every ounce of strength and determination that we had, and he, in the course of a few years, transformed us from hesitant, clumsy little marionettes into gymnasts.

The Roltschs' gym was built into their basement, and to get to it, you had to walk down a steep, spiraling sidewalk that curled around the house and led straight to the door of the upper deck of the gym. Up there, we all pulled off our sweat suits and socks, tossed our shoes against the wall, and scampered down the thirteen planked stairs onto the floor mats below. The gym had its own smell which I came to automatically associate with the sweat of grueling workouts and the sweet, paralyzing exhaustion that always accompanied them.

I quickly became addicted to the anesthetic effect of the draining workouts, so much so that whenever I entered the gym, even before

I had stripped down to my leotard, I could feel tender, invisible fingers gently massaging and stretching my muscles in preparation for the next two hours of leap, tumble, and swing.

My first victory in gymnastics came when I turned my first cartwheel. Some one had tried to show me what a cartwheel looked like by using a Barbie doll, but I could not understand. In my eight-year-old mind, I was a little girl, not a doll, and I was not able to imagine my body manipulating itself the way the doll moved in the hands of my coach. For weeks, maybe even months, I tried mechanically to turn a cartwheel, putting down slowly first one hand, then the other hand, then one foot, then the other foot. I felt like a long-limbed gorilla slapping the mat with my hands and clumping with my feet as I tried to force my body to turn itself properly.

Then, one day it happened without my even trying; in fact, that must have been why it happened. All of a sudden, I found myself sliding smoothly through the air and landing in the same position I'd started in. I knew as soon as I landed that this was how a cartwheel was supposed to feel. I still did not understand exactly how I'd done it, much less what it looked like, but I did know what one felt like, and that was all that mattered.

The next challenge was to train myself to do a straight cartwheel, so I turned wheel after wheel using the crack between the mats as my guiding line. It took the horse a while, but finally it learned to pull the cart straight down that line.

The "floor ex," short for floor exercise, was my second favorite event. I didn't like doing balance beam because I couldn't keep myself from falling off; and, because I could not run straight down the 30-foot runway to the vault, I could not build up enough power to hurl myself over it. But, the "floor" (I especially liked its more modern version, the spring floor, that was carpeted and bounced slightly when you fell on it) for me consisted of gravity, the expansive flatness, and the infinite space above it through which I could leap and twist and somersault to my soul's content.

Truly, to be off the ground, buoyed up in air, restrained by nothing, and surrounded by an exhilarating nothingness for just an instant, is the sweetest liberation I have ever known. For that reason, my favorite "move" on the floor was the double front handspring, because keeping my body in constant motion during those three to four seconds electrified me every time I did one. I would launch onto my right foot as though I were skipping, then after my left foot hit the ground once, I lunged forward and boxed the floor with open palms as my feet sailed in an arc over my head and landed in front of my hands which sprang from the floor rocking me forward into a standing position once again. I would then repeat the move, except this time without the skipping start, because the momentum of the first handspring catapulted me into the second handspring.

For the record, I admit that throughout my six years as a gymnast, I had to work extremely hard at being both flexible and graceful. However, when it came to the floor

*Tonia L. Valletta: Ready for whatever
the future holds!*

and the uneven bars, I was the queen of brute strength and aggression: the two bars levitated in space, the gravity, the nothingness, and the expansive flatness were all my subjects, and I forced them to work as hard for me as I did for them.

My favorite event, as well as my best, was the uneven bars. I received my highest score ever, an 8.25, doing a class four bar routine. Other coaches worked with me on floor, beam, and vault; but when it came time to work on the uneven bars, Mr. Roltsch was my coach to the exclusion of all other coaches and assistant coaches. When he realized that I loved the bars the best and was strong and daring enough to take them on, he dedicated himself to the challenge of helping me to perfect my bar routine.

Gradually, yet unmistakably, "the bars" ushered themselves into the center of the gym as I visualized it—and I, the bars, and Mr. Roltsch pressed on toward ultimately unachievable perfection.

At my first gymnastics meet, I did only my bar routine because it was my best and most practiced. I remember that day well. The rest of the team was already at the meet doing their other three routines. It wasn't yet time to join them, so Mom dropped me off at the Roltschs' house. Mr. Roltsch met me at the door and took me through his house and downstairs into the gym. There, he helped me warm up on the bars and run through a few routines so I would be ready at the meet. Then we went back upstairs, I dressed, and we sat outside on his porch drinking lemonade. I don't remember what we said, but I know that I felt loved and protected sitting with Mr. Roltsch on his porch. We then drove to the meet, and I did my routine. I was scared, but I made it through and got a score of 6.65. My coach was happy with that score.

A few years passed, and I turned eleven on May 13, 1985. I was a fifth-grader, and school was almost over. Some time before that, a friend had told me, my Mom, and Mr. and

Mrs. Roltsch, about a national sports competition for the blind that happened every year during the first week of June. This year, "Nationals," sponsored by USABA, the United States Association for Blind Athletes, would be held in Trenton, New Jersey. By now, my bar routine had improved considerably along with my other three routines; I now competed all-around doing all four events in the meets I went to. So, my coach, my Mom, and I talked it over briefly and decided that I should go to New Jersey.

Soon, I was sitting quietly in the back seat of the Roltschs' car as we drove north; my parents followed the next day.

On the morning of the competition, I was more terrified than I had ever been in my entire life. I felt sick to my stomach, and I could hardly swallow the chocolate milk Mr. Roltsch told me I <u>had</u> to drink. All had gone well in practice, but now was the real thing, my one and only chance to prove myself to all those who would be watching, including my parents. Floor, beam, and vault came and went in a haze; I fell off the beam four times, and set a national record with my score on the floor exercise. Then came the uneven bars. I was psyched, I was ready—and I was scared. There was one move in the routine I was particularly worried about. It was the hardest move in the routine, and if I didn't get the timing absolutely right, I would miss it completely.

Perching on the low bar facing forward, I would do a "single-leg shoot through" to straddle the bar, then reverse grip, and raise myself from off the bar to circle swiftly around it. This move was called a "mill-circle catch" because in mid-rotation I would let go of the low bar about 7/8 of the way around to reach for the high bar. If I let go too early or too late, I wouldn't catch the bar, and Mr. Roltsch would have to touch me to keep me from falling. If he touched me, the judges would deduct half a point from my score. We had practiced this move hundreds of times, and I knew I could do it perfectly. But, would I? Or would I clam up and not let go at all?

I was up. I splashed chalk on my hands and positioned myself standing on the mat in front of the low bar. I touched the bar, saluted the judge, and began my routine. It was swift, tight, and powerful. Pausing not even for an instant, I shot my leg through to straddle the low bar, reversed grip, raised myself off the bar, and ... whapp! I had done it: I had caught the high bar. The audience gasped in a hushed voice, and I heard my Dad exclaim in astonishment, for he had never seen me compete before. I finished my routine, and Mr. Roltsch hugged me as the applause raged and surrounded me with its love.

As I stood on the top level of the make-shift platform with one girl standing below me to my right and another below me to my left, I cautiously lifted my hands to my neck and felt the thick, wide ribbons that cascaded down my chest. There were five medals spread out just below my chest: four gold and one silver. I had won the first-place all-around medal, which meant that I was now the reigning national champion blind gymnast. I kept smiling while pictures were snapped of

me with the second and third place winners—
it was so wonderfully easy to smile.

As we all left the gym victoriously, the
medals at my chest began to jingle rhythmically
as I walked. After a few steps, I put my hand
over them to quiet them, because I was afraid
that the people walking with me would think
I was being obnoxious. "Tonia," my friend
exclaimed jubilantly, "take your hand away.
For goodness sake, let those medals jingle!"
The others agreed heartily, so I removed my
hand, and the medals at my chest began to
swing and bounce wildly with a glorious <u>chink</u>
... chink ... <u>chink</u> ...

The blind athlete's competition was my first
encounter with a national organization
involved with blind people. More recently I
have come to be a part of the National
Federation of the Blind. After being urged
by my friends to attend the National
Convention, I decided that the most godly
and appropriate thing for me to do would be
to attend with an open mind and heart. To
my great surprise and delight, as I met one

Federationist after another, I encountered blind people who were friendly, polite, and confident in their own abilities. And I noticed other characteristics of Federationists that impressed me very much. Most notably, I observed a contagious enthusiasm and energy, together with a strong, binding sense of commitment to bettering the position of blind persons in society.

I found myself compellingly attracted to this group of people who shared my enthusiasm and willingness to work hard to accomplish set goals, so I decided to join the National Federation of the Blind and to search for ways to use my own special gifts and abilities to further the independence, goals, and aspirations of all blind people.

There are many ways to let the medals jingle.

Sewing

By Ramona Walhof

Ramona Walhof grew up on a small farming community in rural Iowa. She and her brother and sister were born blind. Yearning for something to do during one long, dull summer, Ramona asked her mother (who was an accomplished seamstress) to teach her to sew. The story that follows is her account of a lifetime of satisfaction and practical good—from hobby, to employment, to family budget-stretcher—gained from this rapidly disappearing art.

Along the way, Ramona (who was widowed in her early 20's) also raised two children, owned and managed a commercial bakery, taught school, and directed employment programs for the blind. Today she operates a very successful public relations business and is President of the National Federation of the Blind of Idaho. She also serves as a national officer in the National Federation of the Blind. Here is what she has to say:

When I learned to sew, I never thought much about blindness. I didn't avoid thinking about blindness. It was a part of me. But when I needed a method to do something that others did visually, I just did what seemed most likely to work. Nobody suggested that blindness should prevent sewing until I knew better.

As I grew older, I came across blind girls and women who had been actively discouraged from doing things I learned as a child. Sewing for me has provided employment, relaxation, challenge, and accomplishment. It has helped me to learn about fabrics, styles, and colors. There are things I never attempted (some because of blindness) but most because of lack of time. Perhaps one day I may still take up some new kinds of sewing such as quilting. I know it would be delightful to do if I ever get to it.

When I was a young child, summers were boring. My brother, sister, and I attended the School for the Blind during the school year. We were very glad to go home at the end of

May each spring, but we didn't have a lot of friends in our home town, and we got tired of not having enough to do. We took swimming lessons, participated in local church activities, helped with cleaning and cooking (washing dishes was the worst), visited with grandparents and cousins. We hauled as many Braille books home from school as we could fit in the car with all our clothes and other possessions. My brother managed to talk our Dad into some ham radio equipment and entertained himself with that. My sister and I generally rationed our books some and got Braille magazines, but there never was really enough to do.

One summer, (the one after my fifth grade year), I decided to try to solve the problem. I announced to my mother with the diplomacy customary for me at the time, "This summer you are going to teach me to sew." My mother had been making clothes for us as long as I could remember. We got some school clothes from stores and from catalogs, but the ones she made were always nice, and we could help decide what they would look like. Several people in our family sew, and my mother had a buttonholer on her machine, so people would bring their garments to our house to do the buttonholes. So it seemed natural for me to want to sew.

My mother didn't resist at all. She responded with a question, "What do you want to make?" I never asked her what she thought about it, but I really don't think she was shocked. Perhaps a little uncertain about some of the techniques. Actually, techniques were not a problem. I told her I wanted to make gym clothes. I figured a few mistakes could be tolerated in gym clothes. I think that neither my mother nor I knew that blindness was much of a factor, so it wasn't.

We decided that the gym shirt should have a plain round neckline with cap sleeves. This was my idea so that I would not have to gather the sleeves and set them in. My mother cut a pattern out of newspaper, designing it from something else she had. I pinned the pattern on the material and cut it out. Then my mother realized that she had forgotten the cap sleeves, so they had to be set in after all. This made the project more complicated for a beginner, but the gym shirt looked great to me. I learned to guide the material through the sewing machine using a quilting guide my mother had. I learned to pin seams and hems closely and remove the pins just before they came to the presser foot. I learned to move the gathers on the gathering thread and put them where they should be when I pinned the gathered piece to the one it needed to be sewed to. Really, it wasn't as hard as I had feared. I wore that gym shirt all through sixth grade. I don't think we ever got to the shorts.

Marking darts could be done with pins or basting threads. There were so many different kinds of darts that it took me some practice to get them all figured out. Gradually, I got so I could judge the size of darts pretty accurately without having to use the marks from the pattern itself.

When we came home for Christmas that year, I made a yellow skirt. It turned out all right, too. This time I used the tissue paper pattern. My cutting technique seemed obvious to me, and my mother never commented on it. Only later did we learn that blind people weren't supposed to be able to cut around tissue paper patterns.

I held the scissors with my right hand the way most people do. I looped my left hand over the top of the scissors with the thumb and fingers opposite each other right at the part of the scissors that did the cutting. If the edge of the pattern was at the top of the bottom scissors blade, I could feel tissue paper on one side and fabric on the other. If the scissors were not right at the edge of the pattern, I would have paper or fabric on both sides of the bottom blade. The more practice I got, the better I got, but even as a beginner, I could cut reasonably well along the edge of the pattern.

Patterns come in an envelope in big sheets, and my mother would cut the pieces apart and trim on the cutting lines. She never really read the instructions to me. Rather, she taught

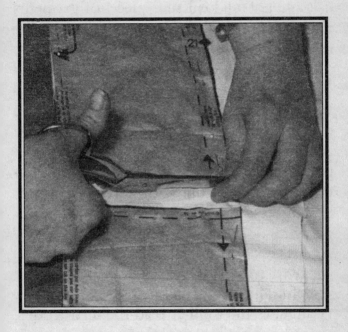

Cutting out the pattern by touch.

me basic concepts about how to set in sleeves, turn down a skirt band over the seam, set in a zipper, assemble and attach a collar, etc. She also taught me to identify pieces of garments by their shapes. Sleeves would tend to be round at one end and square at the other. Blouses and dress tops had big arcs cut out where the sleeves would be attached. The curves at the front and back of slacks and shorts were shaped differently from sleeve curves. The curve at the back was bigger than the curve at the front for slacks patterns, but the curve in the front of the top where sleeves are in-set is bigger than the one at the back.

Much later I learned that the instructions printed with the patterns could often be helpful when taking on a new style of garment. I am sure my mother read the instructions, because she often used them when we were laying out fabric before we cut it out. But we often found better ways to make efficient use of the material than the patterns showed. I don't remember what I made during the summer after my sixth grade year, but I am sure there was something.

In any case when I enrolled in home economics in seventh grade, I already knew some of the basics about sewing. Our teacher was new that year and had no background working with blind girls. Our first project was to make an apron. There was no cutting. Everything was on a straight line and could be torn with the grain of the fabric. The aprons had a blue border at the bottom with a flowered print above. The bands and sashes were straight pieces. The sashes had to be hemmed, and aprons had to be gathered and attached to the bands.

There were eight girls in my class, and most of us could sew a hem fairly straight by the time the aprons were done. The teacher really didn't want us to run a machine without having her present to watch. I disregarded this instruction without too much teacher protest.

I learned about the seam guide in that class. You can buy a little metal hump that screws into the top of the machine cabinet which is better than my mother's quilting guide. For the rest of the first semester our home economics class cooked. Second semester was the real sewing class. My friend and I decided to make tangerine skirts, but they were different patterns.

The teacher's first notion was that she would cut out all the patterns. Unfortunately for her, I was there to object. So I cut out my own pattern. I also offered to help other kids learn to do it. Some of the girls really didn't have much trouble. Some tended to place the fingers of their guiding hand at the end of the scissors instead of where the cutting occurred. They were constantly being warned to be careful not to cut themselves. Since I thought everybody knew better than to close the scissors with fingers between the blades, these warnings seemed unnecessary. Certainly, some of the students were more fearful of scissors than they needed to be. We also learned how to assemble all our different patterns.

When I cut out my blouse, I made an error. I should have laid the back on the fold, but I cut it on the edge of the fabric, thus requiring a seam where there should have been none. If I had not been so determined to do it myself, the teacher doubtless would have found this error before it was done. Some students were much too cooperative in my judgment and did not do as much of the work themselves as they could and should have.

We could all thread a regular needle using a needle threader with a fine wire loop. When the wire loop is in the eye of the needle, the thread is brought through the loop. When the needle threader is removed from the needle the thread passes through the eye. Large eye needles made this easy. Our teacher encouraged basting, but most of us didn't like to do it. We all learned to baste, though, because we were required to baste zippers. We also learned to hem garments with an overcast stitch. It was desirable not to see the thread on the outside of the hem. With practice, some of us got pretty good at this.

Threading the machines presented another challenge. When threading the machine, one needed to pass the thread through several metal or plastic loops. No one had trouble learning where to put the thread, but we would not notice loops of thread that got caught in other places while we were doing the threading.

It took me a while, but I finally realized that if I kept the thread taut from spool to needle while doing the threading, I could tell if there were errors or loops where they should not be. We always blamed the tension if something went wrong, and I feel sure that we did inadvertently turn the dial at the tension sometimes.

With experience, I learned to tell from the stitching itself when the top and bobbin tensions were balanced. My mother was casual about making constructive suggestions about

*Ramona Walhof: Mother, Seamstress,
Businesswoman, Success!*

things like this and more helpful than anyone else before or since. She would tell me what she looked for, and I could try to learn the same information by touch. More often than not it worked. Everyone (including me) tended to rely on somebody's eyesight for certain judgments at first. If a sighted person wasn't conveniently available to help when wanted, this became a nuisance and provided motivation for all of us to develop techniques that a blind person could use independently.

It is surprising for me now to think about how difficult it sometimes seemed to feel proper stitching. If we had expected to be able to do it from the beginning, we all would have found it easier. As it was, this took some time and experience.

I continued to make clothes during vacations and in home economics. I enjoyed the making and the wearing of the clothes. I also enjoyed making things for others, but seldom had enough confidence to do it. I made a shirt for my dad and a baby dress for a cousin, and I think they were OK.

During college I did not have access to a sewing machine and did very little sewing. Shortly after I was married, though, a sewing machine seemed important to have. We bought a cheap one, a portable one that weighed a ton. It was very heavy to lift on and off the dining room table, so it stayed at one end while we ate at the other during many weeks. I usually put it away on weekends.

I took a set of big bath towels that had been wedding presents but were not being used and made my husband a bathrobe. He was pleased and wore it a lot which pleased me. We still have a picture of him sleeping in a recliner in that bathrobe with our first baby on his shoulder also asleep. When I got pregnant, I knew I could save money by making maternity clothes. I did make some, and my mother made me some, too. We didn't spend much. Then, of course, it is even more fun to sew for your children.

Knits were the big thing in the early 70's so I took a short course at the YMCA in stretch and sew. We didn't sew during class.

We took our assignments home, so the teacher had no occasion to worry about blindness. If she didn't explain something, I asked, but this was easy for all. I made pants and a shirt for my daughter who was a toddler and a matching set for my son who was a tiny baby. I also made a shirt for myself. I offered to make my husband a shirt, but it never got done. It was already cheaper to buy t-shirts than to make them.

After my husband died and I returned to work at the Commission for the Blind in Iowa, I was immediately assigned to teach sewing along with Braille. My students all wanted to sew with knits, so the stretch and sew class was far more valuable than I had ever dreamed. Some of my students were beginners, and some had far more sewing experience than I. This concerned me at first, but I found that we could learn from each other in wonderful ways.

Several of my students went home and took up sewing a lot. Others did less but enjoyed it. One young woman had been a professional seamstress in an alterations department for a big store. She chose to make a jacket that had three parallel rows of top stitching for trim that were supposed to be done in three different colors. I cautioned her about this, but that is the kind of thing she liked. I thought that her control as a newly blinded seamstress might not be as good as desirable for something that showy, but it really turned out fine. I cannot say how many students I taught sewing or how many outfits I made for myself and my children during the next several years, but I gained a lot of experience.

It was during that time that people began using machines with cams and other kinds of fancy stitches. These made sewing even more fun! Making decorative items or decorations on clothes was something we <u>had</u> to do. We just couldn't ignore these interesting new sewing machine features.

When my daughter was in second grade, she joined Bluebirds. They were supposed to make red felt vests, and none of the mothers wanted to take on this project. I thought felt vests were not sensible for second graders. One slip of the scissors would be ugly, and felt was expensive. I offered to have the group make skirts at my house. Other mothers thought I was crazy, but agreed. It was simple—use navy blue rectangular pieces of polyester knit fabric. Turn down the top enough to pull three-quarter inch elastic through. Turn up the bottom two inches and sew red rickrack around at the top of the hem. There was only one seam required and no hand sewing. The girls could use the sewing machines if their mothers would let them. The skirts were cute as they could be, and the girls were proud as peacocks.

By the time my daughter was in sixth grade, it was clear to me that she wanted more clothes than I was willing to buy. I told her she could probably have more clothes throughout junior high and high school if she would learn to sew. She was more than eager. She chose to make a three tiered white skirt with purple trim. The gathers on three tiers wore her out, so I helped, but she did the rest. She wore it for her sixth grade graduation and looked great. When she was called to the front for the top award from the school, I had tears and wished one more time that my husband could have been there to share it with us.

Anyway, Laura was a confirmed sewer, although she still had a lot to learn. We began to learn about new kinds of patterns together. While she was in high school, she made casual clothes, but I did the more formal ones. When kids need something for school, you don't always get much notice. When Laura joined the orchestra, she needed a black formal. Her friend's mother knew the right pattern, and I made it. For her first formal dance, I made her a mint green long satin dress with puffed sleeves and an inverted "v" below the bust. She had a good bustline, and the dress looked good on her. She took it to college with her, when the time came.

Now, Laura does more sewing than I do. She got practice during college and made a friend's wedding dress. Today, for me sewing is a hobby, but it is there when needed or wanted.

I love to share this experience with others. It is a way of being creative and busy. One summer I went looking for clothes and just couldn't find much. Before long I switched to shopping in fabric stores and had the clothes I liked. Making a work dress can be done in about the time needed for two shopping trips, and if shopping isn't going well, sewing is more satisfying. I also can make clothes fit the way I want them to. If I ever have grandchildren, there will probably be things to do for them. Time will tell.

If I ever have an opportunity to teach sewing again, I will be much more confident about what projects my students should attempt. One more thing. For a blind person who likes to read recorded books and magazines, sewing is one of those things you can do while reading.

You can help us spread the word...

... about our Braille Readers Are Leaders contest for blind schoolchildren, a project which encourages blind children to achieve literacy through Braille.

... about our scholarships for deserving blind college students.

... about Job Opportunities for the Blind, a program that matches capable blind people with employers who need their skills.

... about where to turn for accurate information about blindness and the abilities of the blind.

Most importantly, you can help us by sharing what you've learned about blindness in these pages with your family and friends. If you know anyone who needs assistance with the problems of blindness, please write:

Marc Maurer, President
National Federation of the Blind
1800 Johnson Street, Suite 300
Baltimore, Maryland 21230-4998

Other Ways You Can Help the National Federation of the Blind

Write to us for tax-saving information on bequests and planned giving programs.

OR

Include the following language in your will:

"I give, devise, and bequeath unto National Federation of the Blind, 1800 Johnson Street, Suite 300, Baltimore, Maryland 21230, a District of Columbia nonprofit corporation, the sum of $_____ (or "____ percent of my net estate" or "the following stocks and bonds:_____") to be used for its worthy purposes on behalf of blind persons."

Your Contributions Are Tax Deductible